The Business of Criminal Law

How to Build a Practice You and Your Clients Will Love

by Joshua S. Baron

Copyright © 2017 by Joshua S. Baron

All rights reserved. This book or any portion thereof may not be reproduced or used in any manner whatsoever without the express written permission of the publisher except for the use of brief quotations in a book review.

Nothing in this book is intended as legal advice. Nor does it create an attorney-client relationship. Consult with your state bar and follow any ethical or professional rules governing law firms before offering legal services.

Contact the author at baron.josh@gmail.com.

Contents

Introduction..4

Part I: Should I be a criminal defense attorney?........10

Part II: How do I get good at criminal defense?........18

Part III: How do I position myself as an expert and charge a premium for my services?...........................56

Part IV: How can I be a happy criminal defense attorney?..65

Conclusion...73

Bonus Chapter: Marketing for Criminal Defense Lawyers..76

Introduction

I was standing in front of the jury that would decide my first jury trial. I had been a prosecutor for only five days and I had spent the first three of those days in human resources orientation. I had no idea that there was so much to learn about retirement investments and avoiding sexual harassment lawsuits. Not only had I never tried a case to a jury before, I had never seen a jury trial. And I was screwing it up. Big time.

It was a refusal DUI. Meaning, the driver refused to blow into the breath machine that would have measured her breath alcohol level. My job was to convince the jury that there was enough evidence that she was impaired without the chemical test to get a conviction. Our main evidence was that, according to the police officer, the defendant had failed the field sobriety tests. The problem was, I couldn't remember the name of the first, and most important field sobriety test.

"Members of the jury, the most important evidence you heard today was the police officer's testimony that the defendant failed the—" Nothing. What was the name of that test? I glanced over my shoulder at the attorney supervising me. She was smiling and shaking her head. My face turned red. This was not how I was hoping my first trial would go. The word was gone. There was no getting around it. In my defense, the name of the test is a mouthful: Horizontal Gaze Nystagmus. But I now know that it is usually a good idea for the prosecutor to remember the name of the most important piece of evidence in his case.

I tried to laugh. "You'll have to excuse me. I forget the name of the test. Maybe you remember the name. It's the one that looks for involuntary eye movement." That probably didn't help my credibility a ton, but the members of the jury looked like they were still listening, so I plunged on. "But the officer testified that that test is highly reliable in his experience. Add that to the fact that the defendant refused to blow into the breath machine, and you have enough evidence to convict beyond a reasonable doubt."

My face and ears burned. I was sure that the jury would acquit and my boss would realize he'd made a mistake in hiring me. No one was more surprised than I was when the jury came back with a guilty verdict.

I tell you that story for a couple of reasons. First, even though I was mortified that I flubbed the closing argument so badly, that trial changed my life. It might not sound possible from the story, but I loved the whole process of a criminal jury trial. The thrill of questioning witnesses, making objections, and responding to the defense attorney's arguments was an incredible feeling. I wanted more of it. I spent a year as a prosecutor and then left to start my own criminal defense firm and I've been in court fighting and trying cases ever since. I'm not sure I would have ever realized how much I love criminal law and trial if I hadn't tried being a prosecutor.

The second reason I tell that story is to show you where I started. I am a successful criminal defense attorney. I have won not-guilty verdicts and dismissals in dozens of serious felony and misdemeanor cases. I have successfully defended homicide, rape, child abuse, and drug distribution cases. Over the last eight years of practice, I have earned millions of dollars in fees. It might be immodest, but I am at the point where I can look at my clients in the eye and tell them with all sincerity, "There is no one who can do a better job at this case. If you want the best possible outcome, you should hire me." I have the evidence to prove it. But I didn't start out as some savant. It took years of practice and making mistakes. I did my best, but I wasn't perfect the first time I cross-examined a hostile witness or conducted a preliminary hearing or selected a jury. I am much better at those things now. And I'm still working at getting better.

The purpose of this book is to help you start wherever you are and create a criminal defense practice that you and your clients love. If you are a seasoned criminal defense lawyer with hundreds of trials under your belt, but you're sick of running from hearing to hearing putting out fires and getting paid less than you're worth, this book will help you create a practice you will love. If you are in law school or just graduating and the prospect of doing document review until three in the morning at a big corporate firm sounds like death, this book will help you chart a different, better path.

This isn't a cookie cutter recipe to create a carbon copy franchise of my firm. This book will outline a process that will let you create a new firm that has never existed before and will never exist if you don't create it. Your clients are waiting for you to do it. You will be very glad you did.

This book is divided into four parts. Each answers a different question.

> Part I: Should I be a criminal defense attorney?
>
> Part II: How do I get good at criminal defense?
>
> Part III: How do I position myself as an expert and charge a premium for my services?
>
> Part IV: How can I be a happy criminal defense attorney?

I hope this book is helpful to you. I hope you can learn from my experiences. If you have questions or ideas or comments about the book, please email me at baron.josh@gmail.com. I'd love to help you and encourage you to create a firm that reflects your unique talents and personality. There is nothing I like more than having good conversations with interesting people, so don't be shy about emailing me.

Part I: Should I be a criminal defense attorney?

Too many lawyers are miserable. I was almost one of them. I went to law school for some stupid reasons. I was a history major in undergrad and none of the big history firms were hiring, so I knew I needed to go to graduate school. There is math on the GRE and the GMAT, but no math on the LSAT, so I took the LSAT, got a good score and went to law school. I had no plan on what I was going to do when I graduated. I felt immense pressure to graduate in the top 10% of my class so that I could get "the best job" at a big firm in L.A., New York, or Chicago.

I did internships during law school and during the summers. I hated them all. I did corporate compliance at Baker & McKenzie in Argentina. Hated it. I did some employment litigation for a medium-sized firm in Southern California. Everyone was super nice, but I hated it. I did complex bad faith insurance litigation with a two-attorney firm in Claremont, California. The two attorneys couldn't have been nicer. But I hated it. By the time I started my first job out of law school doing real estate litigation in Park City, Utah, I was convinced that going to law school had been a huge mistake and I was destined to hate every job I had for the rest of my career.

Luckily, that job in Park City was so miserable, I had to leave. I'm going to tell you a story about how awful that job was. You won't believe it and I don't blame you. If I hadn't lived through it, I wouldn't believe it either.

The Park City job was miserable for a lot of the normal reasons. The firm didn't have enough work for me, so I spent my days reading the Washington Post from cover to cover every day and begging the other attorneys for work. I didn't meet my billable requirement once while I was there. Not because I was lazy, but because there just wasn't enough work to go around. Also, I hate civil litigation. No one grants continuances. Opposing counsel was always yelling at me. It was boring, when I had work it was stressful, and I was overall miserable from the very first day.

Those are normal problems with normal jobs, and I might have stuck it out. But my boss made me bring every scrap of paper that I wrote to him for approval before it was filed or sent to a client. If I wrote a letter that said, "We received the following documents on your case," my boss would read the letter with a red pen and change as much of it as possible.

One day, I was waiting outside his office so that I could force him to read something that urgently had to go out. He had me follow him into his office and I sat on a chair and waited while he chewed on his lip, read my memo, and spilled blood red ink on the words that I had been crafting painstakingly for days. While I waited, I examined the framed copy of his LSAT score. The first time I met my boss, during the interview process, he had told me he got a perfect score on the LSAT, and the proof was right there on the wall in a gold frame.

What happened next is extraordinary. After he had been reading for a few minutes, my boss loudly and obviously farted. There is no polite way to say it. There was no mistaking the sound or the overpowering odor. That's a weird thing to do, but guys are weird and gross. The crazy thing is, that my boss didn't say anything about it. He didn't apologize. He didn't make a joke about it. He didn't accuse me of creating the offensive odor. He just kept marking up my memo as if nothing had happened. When I got out of that office, I told one of the other attorneys what had happened and he said the same thing happened to him and basically every other male attorney at the firm.

So, that firm wasn't a good fit. I was desperate. I was married and my wife wanted kids, so going back to school would be tough. But I was close to deciding that I didn't want to be a lawyer. I decided to try the thing that was the most different from what I had previously done and sent a resume to the Salt Lake City Prosecutor's Office. For some reason, they hired me. I am so glad they did. What a waste it would have been to spend the rest of my career fighting about deposition dates with Park City attorneys and getting farted on by my boss. I would never have realized how much I love criminal trials.

I firmly believe that everyone has unique talents. That means that if you don't discover and develop those talents, no one else has them and the world will miss out on them. So have the courage to keep looking if you haven't found your niche yet. Take a risk. Send out a resume. Do an internship. Advertise for something you don't do so you can see if you like it. If your passion is criminal defense, this book will be very helpful to you. But if it isn't, don't stop looking until you find it.

Make sure you recognize it when you find that thing that you were meant to do. Just because you are good at something doesn't mean you should spend your career doing it. If you don't get excited about it, if you don't think about it while you're going to sleep, if you don't admire the people who are masters at it, it's not the right thing for you. Keep looking. At the same time, you should not expect to master the thing you were put on earth to do easily or quickly. Michael Jordan was a ferocious competitor in practice. He was born with extraordinary talent, but it was raw. He had to develop it. It would have been a waste of his talent if he had spent his whole career teaching piano. That is not what he was put on earth to do. But if he had given up basketball because he didn't immediately and naturally have a post-game, he would never have won six NBA championships.

It is tempting to think you can find that perfect fit by reading career books and taking aptitude tests. There is nothing wrong with thinking carefully about your life plan. But there is no substitute for trying things. In my case, I would never have seriously considered criminal defense. There is nothing that I knew about my personality or about the criminal defense process that would have made me think they would fit.

In Spanish, there are two different words that can be translated as "to know" in English: saber and conocer. Saber means to know something intellectually. For example, I knew that I would love my kids before I met them. I knew that playing the guitar involved plucking or strumming strings before I could play. I know that Barack Obama likes basketball even though I have never met him.

Conocer is experiential knowledge. I know my wife. I know a list of facts about her, but I know her in a way that I cannot communicate to you by telling you all the facts I know about her. I know how to play guitar in a way that I cannot explain to you if you have never played the guitar. I know about fatherly love because I have experienced it.

Even though I knew that law school would be hard, I didn't know how hard it was until I experienced it. I knew that corporate compliance involved understanding governmental regulations and helping my client comply with them. But I didn't know what that was like until I did it. I knew (saber) that criminal defense involved using procedures like cross-examination, preliminary hearings, and trials to protect people charged with crimes. But I didn't know (saber) that I would love it until I learned about it by experience (conocer). So, don't fall into the trap of analyzing all of your options for so long that you never try stuff. I'm positive that you will hate things that seem like they are logical fits and that you will love things that seem not to make sense.

It's worth it to keep looking because finding your passion is about finding out who you really are. It's about finding the environment where you can be your best and truest self. You can be a good person if you never find your passion. But you will be missing out and the world will be poorer. So keep looking until you find it. Then hold onto it and create things the rest of us would never even think of.

Part II: How do I get good at criminal defense?

It's 9:30 p.m. on a weekday and I'm sweating in the back of a dirty club in West Valley City, Utah. I've been listening to wannabe standup comics for hours. Most of them are terrible. So bad that you get a sympathy panic attack as they self-immolate on the stage.

The emcee calls my name.

Little did I know that the next two minutes would be the worst two minutes of my life.

I stand on the stage and squint into the spotlight. They told me it would be bright, but I didn't realize it would be blinding. I can't see a thing. There are shadows of people sitting in the first row, but nothing beyond that.

"This is my first time doing standup," I say into the microphone. "And I feel left out because nobody offered me any cocaine."

I get a solid laugh. That line occurred to me like five minutes ago. I'm surprised it worked. I go into my prepared material. I mess up the premise. I try to correct myself. It's taking too long. I try to find the punch line. What was this joke about? I forget. It's long and complicated. I'm going too fast.

Silence from the audience. Silence.

I bail on the first joke and start a second joke, but I mix things up again. There's no saving me now. I hurriedly clip the mic back into its stand and run off the stage. I hear the emcee saying something about how hard your first time is. I'm guessing he'll turn it into a losing your virginity joke, but I'm out the door too quickly to hear.

A couple of friends came to see me. I should not have invited them. They follow me into the parking lot. They tell me, "You did good." I did not do good.

One of them videoed it using his iPhone. I ask him to email it to me. He turns pale and shakes his head. He makes excuses. "I'm not sure I can figure it out. The file is probably too big to email."

Those two minutes of video are on my computer right now. I have tried to watch it four or five times since the night in question. I have never made it to the end. If I am ever nominated to be Secretary of State or head of the Bureau of Indian Affairs, that video will be leaked and my political career will be over.

I had secretly wanted to be a standup comedian for years. It took me months to work up the courage to sign up for that open mic night once I found out it existed. I wrote and I wrote and I practiced. And yet, it was still the worst two minutes of my life.

So, my standup career is on hold. Maybe one day I'll have the courage to try again. I might be the next Jerry Seinfeld. Or I might be a dude who wanted to be Seinfeld but ended up forcing his audience to question the utility of their existence while they begged for the experience to be over. Maybe the CIA can use the video to interrogate captured ISIS operatives. "Turn it off! I'll tell you anything."

In other words, it didn't go well and HBO hasn't offered me a standup special yet. How do you go from being so bad at something people will pay you to stop doing it to being an expert? How does anyone get good at standup comedy? How can you become a great criminal defense attorney?

Well, the short answer is practice. But the longer answer is that it takes a certain kind of practice to get really good at anything. In *Outliers*, Malcolm Gladwell makes the case that when people get enough practice, they have the ability to become experts. He popularized the 10,000-hour rule. The 10,000-hour rule posits that you need 10,000 hours of careful practice to become an expert. While 10,000 hours of practice are great, it takes a certain kind of practice to become an expert. It takes a type of high-quality practice psychologists call "deliberate practice." You can practice something for 10,000 hours without becoming an expert if you aren't engaging in this type of focused, effortful practice.

Elements of Deliberate Practice

Deliberate practice has been studied in sports, music, chess, and medicine. In a 2011 study, researchers studying medical students outlined three elements of deliberate practice:

1. Repetitive practice
2. Rigorous skills assessment
3. Specific, informative feedback

The first element is intuitive. Of course we need to repeat the skill to practice it. The second and third elements of deliberate practice, rigorous skills assessment and specific informative feedback, are harder to implement. How do you get rigorous assessment of your ability to make a closing argument or conduct a direct examination or negotiate a plea bargain? How do you get specific informative feedback on your client interviewing skills?

Educational psychologists are convinced that effective feedback is essential to mastering skills. And yet, there is little assessment or feedback in the practice of law. That leads to a lot of very bad lawyering. You can be the exception if you can find effective, rigorous, and informative feedback. My business partner, Yossof Sharifi, has been the source of the huge majority of the feedback I've received over the last nine years. We talk about our cases constantly throughout the day. He listens to me speak to potential clients, negotiate with prosecutors, and observes me in court. Together we try to define the specific, measurable or articulable objectives we are trying to achieve. For example, instead of saying, "My objective is to win this DUI trial," we try to break that down into smaller manageable objectives. "My goal is to personalize my client during the opening statement." Afterward, we reflect together or provide feedback on whether we achieved our objective. That feedback is most effective when we are both there and can judge whether that happened. But even if we weren't, we meet regularly to do a post-mortem. We try to be very specific about what went well and what could have gone better. Over time, my skills have grown to be much better than I could have anticipated. I know that I would not have been able to develop as much or as quickly without Yossof's feedback.

No feedback mechanism is perfect. But we shouldn't abandon the idea of getting feedback because our measures are not ideal. Instead, we should seek out the best available feedback and measurement. Even if it is only writing in a journal about what you are working on and trying to gauge improvement, that will be better than no feedback at all. If your ambition is to be the best criminal defense attorney you can possibly be, you have to do everything you can to get feedback you trust and can act on.

How do I get enough practice?

You have to get a lot of practice to become an expert at anything. It might not take Malcolm Gladwell's 10,000 hours, but you have to put in the time and get enough repetitions to master the skills necessary to be a great criminal defense lawyer.

You can get that practice in a couple of different ways. One way is to get a job where someone else pays you to learn. You might work as a public defender. I worked for a year as a prosecutor. You might find a job as an associate for a criminal defense firm. If you were making a pro and con list about working for someone else, the security of someone more experienced and successful paying your salary would be in the pro column. Hopefully, they will provide some training and mentoring. On the con side, you will be learning to practice the way they practice. It will be hard to develop your own personal style. Your employer will probably give you the worst clients and the most mundane tasks at first.

In my opinion, the best way to get enough practice to become an expert criminal defense lawyer is to go out on your own and do it. In Part III, I will talk about how you can position yourself as a highly paid, well-respected expert. But you have to pay the price to gain that expertise. You have to handle dozens or hundreds of cases, deliver great results for your clients, and carefully practice your skills along the way. Most people look at this as a chicken and egg problem. "I can't get clients until I'm an expert, but I can't develop into an expert until I have clients." But your lack of expertise is actually an opportunity.

If you go into an interview with a potential client who is trying to decide between you and another lawyer who has worked as a criminal prosecutor, a judge, and a defense attorney for thirty years, they will probably go with your competitor. At this stage in your career, you can't compete by comparing quality or experience. It would be a lie to say that you could deliver the same results as that veteran with 30 years of experience. But some people are not in the position to choose between the two best lawyers available. Some have to decide between hiring a lawyer and representing themselves or being assigned a public defender. Those clients can't afford the 30-year veteran. So you aren't competing against the veteran. You are competing against the option of not hiring an attorney.

When Yossof and I started our firm, we positioned ourselves as the Walmart of lawyers. We didn't pretend to have experience we didn't have. But we said, "You thought you couldn't afford an attorney. But you actually can. Wouldn't you rather have an attorney you choose and trust than have one randomly assigned to you or represent yourself?" Our prices were upsettingly low. For most misdemeanors, we would take $100 to get started. Some of those clients never made another payment. Yossof took a sex abuse case for a flat fee of $2,500 and then told me to work on it. Even at that time, $2,500 for a serious felony was way too low a price. We took $6,000 for my first serious rape charge and that included the trial fee. I was embarrassed to ask for so much money and then I spent countless hours and won a not guilty verdict at trial.

Those clients were giving me much more than those low fees, though. They were giving me experience. I did my best, but I made mistakes. Those clients were patient. I hadn't lied to them about who I was. We kept our expenses as low as possible so that we could offer fees lower than anyone else. We represented hundreds of clients and we learned invaluable lessons along the way.

Think of this phase in the development of your criminal practice as your internship. You are getting a Ph.D. in criminal defense the only way you can: by handling lots of criminal defense cases. Take everything you can. Drive to courthouses no one else will drive to. Charge ridiculously low prices and do great work. You will grow your skills, build confidence in your own abilities, and build a reputation that will serve you for decades.

I did a hybrid of these two approaches. I worked for a year as a prosecutor without any plan to become a criminal defense attorney. But that year as a prosecutor prepared me to go out on my own and showed me how much I love criminal work. Personally, I couldn't have gone straight out on my own and started my practice after I left the firm in Park City. My confidence was shot and I had no idea where to start. I didn't know anyone I could ask for advice. I needed that year as a prosecutor to start to develop my skills before I had the confidence to start my own thing. If you have that confidence now, then start your own firm as soon as possible. Too many people put it off for years and then regret the time they've lost. Take the leap and start experimenting. The sooner you find your niche and your style, the happier and more productive you will be.

What skills should I practice?

You have to decide where your time and energy will be best used. I'm sure it would be helpful to memorize the text of every one of the Federal Rules of Criminal Procedure, but it wouldn't be the best use of your time because they are so easy to look up. In my experience, there are three skills that are most important to criminal defense attorneys: (1)

cross-examination, (2) client interviewing, and (3) negotiation. If you enjoy those three skills and are naturally good at them, you are more likely to enjoy being a criminal defense lawyer and to be successful. But even the most naturally talented lawyer will have to practice them deliberately to achieve mastery.

I don't list those three skills in any particular order. They are all three essential. For example, you will be a bad negotiator if you are not confident in your ability to cross-examine effectively. You will also be a bad negotiator if you haven't taken the time in a client interview to identify your client's needs and priorities. You can be a great criminal defense lawyer if you are bad at legal research. It is good to be good at research, but you can outsource it or get around it. But for me the three skills of cross-examination, client interviewing, and negotiation are the essential criminal defense abilities. Incompetence in one will sink your practice.

Cross-Examination

On paper, it was a tough case. My client had made a partial admission and the alleged victim was on board to testify. She sat on the witness stand across from me and my client sat behind me in a jail jumpsuit wearing handcuffs and leg irons. I was halfway through my cross-examination. My questions went something like this:

"So, you were standing next to your parents in the kitchen when he abused you?"

"Yes. They were standing right next to me."

"And they didn't notice anything?"

"No. Nothing."

"Did you cry out or say anything?"

"No. I was too scared."

"And as far as you could tell, no one seemed to notice what the defendant was doing?"

"No."

The prosecutor was a tough lady who hated giving deals. But after that preliminary hearing, she offered a misdemeanor based on my client's admission that all of this happened in a public place and no one else noticed. My client got out of jail. That cross examination saved him from a life sentence.

I hate CLE. But I've been to one good one. Terence MacCarthy taught a CLE in Salt Lake on cross-examination. It was a one-day seminar and I probably took it in 2007. But I think about what he taught me every time I go into an evidence hearing. Cross is my favorite part of being a criminal defense attorney. I love doing it and I think I have a natural talent for it.

Cross-examination is an essential skill for defense attorneys because one of our main functions is poking holes in the credibility and in the stories of prosecution witnesses. Our main tool for doing that is cross-examination. It is not uncommon for me to do a jury trial in which I do not call a single witness. So I don't get to do any direct examination. I have to introduce all of the evidence I want and develop my whole theory using the prosecution's witnesses in cross-examination. It is the most essential courtroom skill a defense attorney has.

Direct examination is easy. Anyone can stand at a podium with a notepad and stacks of documents and ask, "What happened next?" over and over again without listening to the answers.

The trick of direct examination is preparing your client or your witness in advance to be able to tell their story with relatively little prompting and to avoid the parts they don't want to emphasize. Pretty easy.

Cross-examination is hard because it's adversarial. You are almost always questioning someone who doesn't like you and wants to disagree with you. Unlike on *Law & Order*, criminal witnesses rarely have a crisis of conscience on the stand and confess to the crime. They've had a long time to prepare and to think about what they're going to say.

For me, the biggest mistake criminal defense attorneys make on cross-examination is this: they don't know what they're trying to do. You have to have a meaningful and achievable goal so that you can tell if what you're doing is likely to produce the outcome you want. If we agree that in most trials it is unlikely that the witness will recant all of their testimony under the pressure of cross-examination, then what is our goal? According to MacCarthy, and my experience has proven him to be right, we should have two primary goals: (1) be in control during the questioning, (2) tell a story, and (3) avoid looking like a jerk. It's hard to do all three at the same time, but when you do, it's a beautiful thing.

Most lawyers focus on being in control during cross. They learned in law school that you should ask leading questions, ask questions you know the answers to, and be the star of the show on cross. It's easy to do those things by being a jerk and belittling the witness. It is hard to do those things while telling a story and avoiding looking like a jerk.

When I started my firm, my law partner and I went to a friend of ours who is a criminal defense attorney for some advice. He said, "Never take a case that involves an emotional female victim." To him, it wasn't worth the aggravation of cross-examining a sympathetic and emotional female victim. So his advice was to avoid those cases. I think part of what he meant was that it is too hard to avoid looking like a jerk when you are cross-examining those witnesses. Yossof and I did not follow that advice. We have worked on many cases involving emotional female victims. We have been successful in those cases because we've learned to be in control and tell a story during cross-examination without looking like a jerk.

And we have Terence MacCarthy to thank for that ability. Whether you decide to take cases involving emotional and sympathetic victims or not, you have to learn to cross examine effectively to be a great criminal defense attorney.

If you get the chance to go to a CLE MacCarthy offers, take it. He's great. If you can't do that, buy his book, *MacCarthy on Cross-Examination*. It's almost $100 on Amazon right now, but it's worth it. It is the bible of cross-examination in our firm. You will win more cases using effective cross-examination than any other courtroom technique. It is worth it to master the technique of cross-examination.

Client Interviewing

Like cross-examination, client interviewing can be difficult for attorneys because they don't know what they're trying to do. They don't understand the objective. In an initial consultation with a potential client they think the goal is to get the client to pay them money. In subsequent interviews with their client, they think the goal is to gather evidence that will help the case. It's nice when clients pay you and it's great when they can point you toward helpful evidence. But those goals look at client interviewing from the perspective of the lawyer and ask what the lawyer can get out of those interactions. You'll be a much better client interviewer if you can really think about things from the perspective of your client.

Why does a potential client call you? What do they need? Why would they hire you rather than someone else? Most attorneys feel that their clients hire them because they want the best possible outcome in their case for the lowest possible price. That is true, but it is a small part of the story. I believe that clients call us because they have an enormous problem that is keeping them up at night and they want someone to take that burden off their shoulders. At the end of the day, most clients are not in a position to evaluate whether you are a good lawyer or not. It's not because they are stupid. It is legitimately difficult to evaluate lawyers. So instead of evaluating your skill as a lawyer, they have to look at something else. They ask, "How does this lawyer make me feel? Am I more or less anxious about this problem after we speak? Does my lawyer care about me? Is my lawyer motivated to solve this problem for me?" Your clients can't tell how good you are, but they can tell how you make them feel. So the first object of client interviewing is helping the client trust you and feel comfortable that you can and will take care of their problem.

When I first started my firm, I was insecure about my skills. I was 25 years old, but I probably could have passed for 16. For years, bailiffs would tell me I couldn't pass the bar into the courtroom because they assumed I was too young to be a lawyer. I got used to showing my Bar identification card and being teased for looking like Doogie Howser. Almost every client I met with asked, "How old are you?"

I tried to compensate for my insecurity and young-looking appearance by telling the clients about my skills. I would tell them how many trials I had won or how many cases I had handled or the kinds of training I had received. I would explain my likely strategy to them in detail and explain complicated evidentiary and procedural issues to them to prove my expertise. What I realize now is that they were asking my age because they wanted to know if they would be able to trust me with their case. They were feeling the same anxiety I was feeling about being too young and too inexperienced. It's not bad to list your credentials at times. It can be a good idea to sketch out a possible strategy. But the reason we share those credibility indicators and plans is so that the clients will feel comfortable. They need to be able to trust you.

The second object of all client interviewing is understanding the client. You can't tell your client if they should go to trial, accept a deal, postpone their case, or resolve it quickly if you don't understand them and their priorities. Take a simple DUI as an example. You might get two DUIs with similar facts that must be approached completely differently depending on the client's plans and priorities. For example, one client might live in an urban area with lots of public transportation and a really good job. For that client, avoiding jail time might be the highest priority. A driver license suspension might not be the end of the world because there are plenty of buses.

But another client who has a commercial driver license and a lot of vacation time saved up might not care about serving jail time but need to keep their license to be able to continue to live and provide for their family.

Once I have learned the basic legal facts of a client's case, I have found that the following questions help clients express their concerns and priorities:

> What are your plans for the future?
>
> How will this case affect your family?
>
> How will this case affect your job?
>
> I'm sure you want to get the best possible outcome in this case, but is there something in particular that most concerns you about it?

I have been surprised to learn that certain clients are planning to go back to school, start a new business, face deportation, care for disabled family members, or have security clearances. Understanding my clients' dreams for the future and priorities for their cases has helped me find creative solutions that meet their needs. When your clients trust you enough and you take the time to understand their concerns, you can give them the best possible chance of achieving the outcomes they need.

Establishing trust and understanding will pay off huge dividends down the road in their case. If your clients trust you, they will be more likely to tell you what really happened. They are more likely to accept your advice about what they should do. They are less likely to be anxious throughout the case. When your clients trust you, they are more willing to pay your fees, recommend you to a friend, and write you positive reviews online.

Attorneys are more than contractors and problem solvers. We are counselors to our clients. We have to treat them as individuals and earn their trust so that they will accept and act on our advice. Client interviewing isn't a courtroom skill, but it will allow you to make the right decisions in court and in the leadup to court hearings so that you can help your clients get the outcomes they need.

Negotiation

Negotiation is the last skill an excellent criminal defense attorney needs to develop, but it is at least as important as client interviewing and cross-examination. The huge majority of cases resolve without trial. In my experience, it is something like 95% of cases. And most of those resolve with plea bargains. So, for 95% of your clients, your trial skills won't directly affect the outcome of their case. You might cross-examine a witness during a motion hearing or preliminary hearing. And if you get a reputation as an incompetent trial lawyer, you'll get worse offers. But a full trial is surprisingly rare in criminal defense. For most of your clients, the best thing you can do is develop your negotiation skills.

A big part of effective negotiation is client interviewing. You will learn about your clients' priorities and help set their expectations in the client interview. You will need that to negotiate effectively.

As with cross-examination and client interviewing, too many lawyers fail to understand the object in negotiation. "The goal is to get the best deal for my client, right?" True. But that is also too narrow a view. An effective negotiator's goal is to understand their negotiating partner so well they'll be able to find creative ways to meet both their own goals and those of their partner.

That sounds like hippy, utopian talk. I understand. But the best negotiation experts in the world look for win-win solutions to negotiation problems, not win-lose solutions. Many of my clients are in absolutely no position to go to trial. I had a client who had broken into a cell phone store using a blowtorch. Once he was inside, he was clearly visible on security cameras stealing cell phones. He was stopped by police not far from the store where they found about 100 cell phones in his car. And he confessed that he had robbed the store. Pretty grim facts for trial. On top of that, he was not a U.S. citizen and any kind of deal involving a plea to burglary would result in almost certain deportation.

I obviously had very little negotiation leverage. I couldn't go in and threaten the prosecutor. He knew those threats would be empty. Unfortunately, it was a prosecutor I didn't know particularly well. The first time I met with him, I asked questions and tried to listen very carefully. I asked, "What do you want to see happen in this case? What is most important to you?" The prosecutor said that he wanted restitution for the store owner. He also said that he had to be able to tell the store owner that my client had gone to jail for a significant period of time. We were able to find a solution that met my client's need to avoid a deportable offense and met the prosecutor's need to show the victim that justice had been served.

A generic good deal would not have achieved my client's objectives. That same deal would have been less valuable to the prosecutor because it would not have resulted in a quick payment of restitution to the victim. We were able to find a win-win solution because we listened to each other.

I am fortunate to have seen these negotiations from both sides — from the prosecutor's perspective and the defense lawyer's perspective. When I was a prosecutor, there was a defense lawyer who was recognized throughout the state for being an expert in the cases he handled. No one knew more about these cases or had more cutting-edge arguments to win them. Unfortunately, every prosecutor I knew hated him. He had a negotiating style that was abrasive and frustrating. He filed motions in cases long before a meaningful negotiation had taken place. Once, I had a case against him on a busy pretrial conference calendar. I circled that case and gave him one of the worst offers of my short prosecutorial career. The defense lawyer rejected the offer, but set it for a pretrial conference a few weeks later. When I picked up the file again and saw my offer, I was embarrassed. I realized that I was punishing his client because of how I felt about him. I made him a reasonable offer and he took it.

This defense lawyer had amazing technical skills, but my first reaction and the first reaction of many other prosecutors I knew, was to give him a worse offer because of his approach to litigating and negotiating his cases. I am confident that some of his clients got worse deals because of the way he treated prosecutors. I'm certainly not saying that you can't litigate your cases and advocate forcefully for your clients, but you will do your clients a great service if you learn to negotiate effectively.

Negotiation is a difficult skill to master because it is difficult to receive accurate feedback. I was very fortunate to learn negotiation in law school form a true expert. Gerald Williams literally wrote the book on legal negotiations, taught at Harvard, and was a fellow at the International Legal Center in Afghanistan. I took two classes from him. The first was an introduction to legal negotiation and the second was advanced negotiation. Those are some of the classes that I think about the most in actual practice.

During our advanced negotiation class, we spent very little time learning about the nuts and bolts of effective negotiation. Instead, we spent all our time looking for ways to measure negotiation skill and design methods to get better. We found that by breaking the complex skill of negotiation into specific and well-defined sub-skills, we were able to improve. If you feel you are not an expert negotiator, take heart. Very few people start out as naturally effective negotiators. It is a skill that can be learned and developed.

Anyone who is serious about learning to negotiate effectively as a criminal defense lawyer should read *Getting Past No* by William Ury and *Getting to Yes: Negotiating Agreement Without Giving In*, by Roger Fisher, William Ury, and Bruce Patton.

Those were the main textbooks in the negotiation classes I took from Gerald Williams. Without trying to fully summarize those seminal works, here are the most important lessons I learned from those books, from Professor Williams, and from my law practice: (1) Make sure you know what you want, (2) Be prepared, (3) Listen carefully to the other side, and (4) Be bold.

Make sure you know what you want.

Too often our clients are vague about the outcome they want. "I want to keep my license," they might say at the beginning of a DUI case. But if you take the time to unpack that desire, you might learn that their real desire is to keep their job. They are afraid they will get fired if they can't drive for a few months. But the bigger obstacle to keeping the job might be jail time. Often there are ways to work around a driver license suspension, but the jail time might be a deal breaker for their employer. By identifying their root concern, you can make sure that the outcome you are working for is the outcome that will actually help your client and accomplish what they want.

Sometimes it is easy to discount what our clients say they want. For example, my clients often say, "I just want to get this over with." For a long time, I basically disregarded that. I would say, "If you're patient, I think we can get a better outcome. I don't want you to regret taking the first deal offered for years to come." I still say versions of that to my clients, but I also try to take them seriously when they say they want to get their case resolved quickly. I ask follow up questions like, "How is this case making you feel?" What they might mean is, "I am feeling really anxious about this case. If I take this deal, I hope this anxiety will go away." Sometimes I can help them deal with their anxiety. They might be worried the prosecutor is mad at us for taking an extra month to think about an offer. They might be worried that they'll go to jail when I know that is very unlikely. But sometimes, the anxiety the case is causing is real and debilitating and worse than the difference between the deal we are working for and the offer on the table. In that case, the best thing I can do for my client is to make sure they really want to take it, and then help them accept the plea bargain so that they can move on with their life.

Each of our clients is more different than we realize. When we take the time to find out what they really want, we can shape outcomes that actually meet those needs. The same outcome in a case might be a huge win for one client and a dismal failure for another. When we take the time to carefully listen to each client and to view them as mature individuals who know what they want, we can serve them much better.

Be prepared.

You have to understand the cards you have. You have to have an understanding of what your case will look like if it goes to trial. Negotiation experts say you have to understand your BATNA. BATNA stands for "Best Alternative To Negotiated Agreement." Obviously your best-case scenario is that you convince the prosecutor to dismiss the case against your client. If only that happened more often! But you can't evaluate the prosecutor's offer to do something other than dismiss the case unless you understand your alternatives. Spend some time outside of court thinking through your alternatives.

One of my friends had a tough case where his client was going to have to register as a sex offender for conduct that most people would probably agree doesn't warrant it. The prosecutor wouldn't budge and a trial would be a suicide mission. Most attorneys, including me, would probably tell the client, "You have two options. You can take the prosecutor's crappy offer or you can go to trial and lose. The offer is bad, but it's better than losing at trial. Let's take it." I hate those conversations.

But my friend is a creative son-of-a-gun. He found out that the family of the client knew a state legislator and said, "Let's just change this registry law." So he made some calls, helped draft some language, testified at some committee hearings, and got the registry language tweaked. He looked at the big view of his client's alternatives to a negotiated agreement.

Often in criminal cases, though, your best alternative to a negotiated agreement is really terrible. It can be frustrating to repeatedly tell your clients that their best option is to take a deal that doesn't get them all of what they want or even need. But there are limits to what you can do when the client has confessed, was caught on video, and was found with the stolen property in his car.

A large part of my practice is advising clients who are undocumented immigrants or immigrants who are not yet U.S. citizens. Their cases can be heartbreaking. They've often made mistakes. Some of them are relatively minor, like possessing some marijuana. Some are major. Often there are things we can do to try to keep them from being deported or losing their status.

But sometimes the choice is between serving a long jail sentence and then being deported, or being deported without serving a long jail sentence. In those situations, my job is to help them understand how bad their BATNA is so that they can see the benefit in taking an offer that will have catastrophic consequences. At the end of the day, the client always gets final decision on whether to accept an offer. But they are entitled to our best advice even when that advice is hard to take.

Listen carefully to the other side.

Criminal defense lawyers love to complain about the terrible offers prosecutors are making them. But they rarely stop to think why prosecutors are making those offers. I am lucky to have spent some time as a prosecutor, so it might be easier for me to see things from their perspective. But even if you haven't been a prosecutor, you will serve your clients better if you can see things from the perspective of the prosecution.

Why is the prosecutor making a bad offer? Is her boss mad at her? Is she getting in trouble for making offers that are too generous? Is there an office policy that restricts how low she can go without permission from a supervisor? Or is this a case the prosecutor feels strongly about?

When I was a prosecutor, I handled about 1,200 cases per year. They all ran together and I felt strongly about very few of them. But I always had two or three files on my desk. They were usually domestic violence cases in which I felt the defendant was a really bad guy and I wanted to stop his dangerous behavior. I tried to be flexible in my negotiations on all but those two or three cases. On most DUIs and certain prostitution cases I was restricted by my office's policies. I offered the minimum sentence I had the power to give. But on my personal high-priority list, I was looking for convictions and jail sentences and I wasn't really open to negotiating on those cases.

When I spoke to defense attorneys, it was refreshing to have a lawyer who listened to me carefully or asked good questions about the case. When they asked, "What do you want to see happen in this case? Is there another way we could do that?" we were more likely to find a creative solution that was acceptable to the defendant. This is a version of what negotiators call focusing on interests rather than positions.

The most effective negotiators find ways to meet their own needs or their clients' needs while maximizing the benefits the other side receives as well. In other words, the best negotiations are not zero-sum competitions for a fixed pie. They are creative attempts to grow the pie so that everyone gets more. It's clichéd, but the best negotiations are win-win and both sides get some of what they need and value most.

The only way to know what the other side values most is to listen to them carefully. The other side may not know what they really want. You may need to help them reflect on that. Some of what the other side wants might be a very human need that doesn't relate in obvious ways to the traditional terms of the negotiation. For example, a criminal prosecutor might make an offer involving fines, jail time, probation, and classes. But that prosecutor might be more interested in feeling respected by other attorneys or not looking like a wuss to the judge or co-workers. If you are not listening carefully and looking to understand what the prosecutor really wants, you might spend a lot of time fighting over things that neither side really cares much about. But if you can meet the prosecutor's real need, she might be more likely to reciprocate and give your client and you what you need.

Be bold.

People who ask for more get more. My law partner is living proof of that.

"My client will plead to the DUI if you'll agree to reduce the charge to reckless driving after he successfully completes probation."

The prosecutor thinks for a minute. "Are we allowed to do that?" he asks.

"Why wouldn't we be allowed?" my partner responds.

And the client ends up with a reckless driving charge on his permanent record instead of a DUI.

The worst the prosecutor can say is, "No." Hearing the word "no" can be painful. It might feel like the prosecutor is rejecting you personally. But that's not true. She's just rejecting your proposal.

One reason bold offers might work is because of a cognitive bias called anchoring. When we are making difficult decisions, it is often hard to know what the answer should be. Prosecutors are often in the position of making difficult judgment calls about the appropriateness of an offer. Because our brains are lazy, they look for shortcuts when making difficult decisions. One of the somewhat misguided shortcuts our brains take is using any available answer to substitute for an answer that is difficult to find. For example, Daniel Kahneman and Amos Tversky showed that what appeared to be a randomly generated number could anchor the answers of test subjects. They spun a wheel of fortune that was rigged to stop at the number 65 or 35 and then asked the subjects what percentage of African countries are in the United Nations. The subjects who saw an irrelevant high number guessed a higher percentage than those who saw a lower number.

When you negotiate, if you make a bold offer, it is possible that the person on the other side of the negotiation will anchor to your aggressive offer. For example, I practice in all kinds of criminal cases from serious felonies to low-level misdemeanors. Often, misdemeanor prosecutors are busy and haven't read their files before court. They haven't written down or even thought about their plea offers. I have found that in that situation, an aggressive offer will provoke a more generous offer. If I say, "My client will accept a suspended plea to trespass as an infraction," the prosecutor might not extend that offer, but she might make a more generous offer than she would have otherwise.

Obviously, there is a limit to how bold you should be. If your offers are always unreasonable, prosecutors will stop listening to you. But when you have a legitimate reason to push for a very generous offer, take it. Ask for more than what you think the prosecutor will give. You might be surprised.

If you understand your BATNA, you won't reject a decent offer if it is the best offer the prosecutor will make. But I have gotten great deals for my clients by asking for things I never thought the prosecution would give. Don't be shy. Advocate for your clients!

Part III: How do I position myself as an expert and charge a premium for my services?

This section is probably the most exciting one in the book. This is where your hard work and passion pay off. Because being an expert is awesome. People are willing to pay a premium for the best when they care deeply about quality. Most people care deeply about the quality of their criminal defense lawyer.

Up until now, you have not positioned yourself as an expert because you were still developing expertise. You were not competing with established, experienced attorneys. You were competing against public defenders and people choosing not to hire a lawyer and represent themselves. There will come a point when you need to transition away from a low-cost model. When you do, your life and your practice will dramatically improve.

It took me a long time to understand the value of positioning myself as an expert. My family shops at Walmart. I am used to shopping for the best possible price for the things I buy. I felt uncomfortable charging premium prices because I tend to be what marketers euphemistically call a "value shopper." I compare prices and look for the best deal.

But shopping for a t-shirt or a television is not the same as hiring a criminal defense attorney. Most of the objects we buy are commodities. There is a nearly identical replacement for almost every object we buy. An LG television is very similar to a Samsung television. One might have features we prefer or cost a little more or a little less, but they are essentially the same thing. And once we decide on a brand and a model, we can choose among a long list of retailers who will sell it to us. Whether you buy a Samsung TV from Amazon or Best Buy or Target, the TV is going to look the same.

Lawyers are not commodities and we should not act like we are. Lawyers are counselors and advocates. A lawyer with great courtroom skills who doesn't understand her client will not be able to help the client make effective decisions. The relationship between the client and the lawyer is very personal and cannot be replaced by a giant corporation or an iPhone application.

Once you reach a level of expertise where you can look a potential client in the eye and honestly say, "You don't need to worry about this anymore because I will take care of it for you. I will do everything I can to fix this problem. No one can do a better job on this than I can," you will be offering something very valuable to that client.

The price you set for your services will signal their quality to the client. If you set your prices at public defender rates, your clients will expect to be treated like public defender clients by an attorney with a public defender caseload. I don't say that to knock public defenders. I love public defenders. They do great work. In courts where the public defenders do good work, all of the defendants benefit from more reasonable offers and outcomes. But public defenders often don't have the time to tailor their representation to each client's unique situation. In some areas of the country, they don't have the time or resources to explore every defense and every tactic. If you price your services too low, your clients will expect that level of services. And because they can't really tell if you're doing a good job or not, they will assume you are not doing a good job and file Bar complaints against you.

When you charge premium fees, you signal the quality of your work to your clients. As I said in the section on client interviewing, your clients can't really tell if you're a good lawyer, but they can tell how they feel when they're with you. If they can tell that you are confident in your work and that you believe your work is of the highest quality, they will sleep well at night knowing that they have a great attorney working for them.

Charging premium legal fees is a service to the client and the attorney. That sounds like heresy, but it's true. The client benefits because they can rest knowing that their attorney is invested in their case. An attorney who is getting paid a high fee doesn't want to get fired. They've signaled they really believe they are doing worthwhile work by charging a premium fee. They will return phone calls and diligently pursue the case. The attorney benefits by being able to take fewer cases and focus their attention on each client's needs. Most attorneys went to law school because they want to help their clients. They want to provide excellent service, but the economics of serving enough clients often forces them to provide mediocre service.

You might object, "But that lawyer down the street will take this case for $899 on a payment plan of $100 per month! How can I charge ten times as much?" If you focus your client's attention in the initial interview on price, you can't. But you can help them shift their attention from price to value. Every day, I get phone calls from people who ask, "How much do you charge for my kind of case?" I respond, "I don't know yet because I don't know enough about your case. But if price is the most important thing to you, then you should call someone else. I am much more expensive than other lawyers and I get much better results. I only work with people who really care about getting the best possible results." Some of these potential clients hang up the phone and call someone who charges less and I am thankful to have wasted very little time discussing their case. But more often, they will say, "Well, I want a really good lawyer. I want to get a great outcome."

Think about this: suppose you were charged with a first-degree felony. First degree felonies in Utah carry a maximum sentence of life in prison. Would you hire someone you were confident would do the best possible work on the case, or someone you were less confident in who charged $5,000 less? The people who want to save some money and risk life in prison are not your ideal clients. You want people who care so much and are so invested in getting the best possible outcome, they are willing to make a substantial financial commitment.

When a potential client asks me, "How much do you charge?" I try to help them refocus on value. I'll say, "Before we talk about my fees, help me understand how this case will affect your future. How will it affect your job? How will it affect your family?" They might say something like, "I can't go to school and get the license I want with a felony on my record and I can't take care of my family if I can't get a good job." I'll say, "I can tell you care a lot about your family. I want to help you realize your dream of going back to school and getting that license. I'm confident I can help you have the best possible chance of reaching those goals. I've done it before for my clients and I'm confident I can help you. If this is really important to you, I will make it really important to me. I'm willing to invest my time and my expertise to help you, but I need you to make an investment to make sure I can dedicate myself to fighting for you. My fee will be ($blank). But I know that will give you the best possible chance of going to school, getting your license, and caring for your family. Would you like to work with me?"

More often than you would think, the potential client says, "Yes," and gives me their credit card number over the phone or writes a check in my office.

If some attorney agreed to help that client for free and then did a bad job and lost the case and the client couldn't work or take care of their family, that would be the client's most expensive case ever. Even a fee of $0 is not worth it if the work is bad and the outcome makes it impossible for the client to achieve their dreams. But if you charge a lot of money and help your client stay on track to achieve their goals and dreams, then that is money well spent.

What if they ask you for a guarantee? They might say something like, "($Blank) is a lot of money. How do I know that you'll be able to get my case dismissed?" When my clients ask that, I say, "I don't know that we'll get your case dismissed (or achieve whatever outcome they are most concerned about). I'll know more once I get the police reports and witness statements. But let me tell you about a similar case I handled recently." Then I will tell them a story about a client who came to me with a difficult problem and the result I was able to help them achieve. I can't predict the future for my clients with perfect accuracy, but I can tell them with total honesty exactly what I've done for a different client in the past.

Too many attorneys think about their cases from their own perspective. How much money do I need to charge to stay in business? Will I enjoy working on this case? How much time will I need to spend on it? But when we stop to listen and understand the case from the client's perspective, we're able to provide better services. Ask yourself, "How important is this case to this client?" If the answer is, "Not very important," then they are not a good client. If the answer is, "Super important!" then they will be willing to invest in finding the right lawyer and compensating them in a way that will allow them to give their case the attention it deserves.

Part IV: How can I be a happy criminal defense attorney?

Once you have a practice that you love and your clients love, you will be much closer to having a happy life. You can't be happy if you are stressed out about paying your bills and if you can't provide your family with the necessities of life. But just because you make a lot of money and enjoy your practice doesn't mean you will be happy.

During my first year in law school, Thomas B. Griffith, a judge on the D.C. Circuit Court of Appeals, came to BYU and spoke to the students. Judge Griffith is a hero of mine. He is insightful and I took a class on presidential power from him that shaped how I think about government and the practice of law. But I didn't know him very well when he came to give this talk. My memory is that the talk was supposed to be for first-year students, but lots of people from all years came to hear him because he is kind of a celebrity at BYU Law School.

His speech was surprising—almost shocking. I didn't take written notes and I'm not aware of a transcript, so I am relying on my memory of what he said, but I've thought about it quite a bit in the years since I heard it. His message was, "If you take your law degrees, and move into the world, and use your degrees to make money for yourself, and don't use your money or your degree to bless other people, you will go to hell."

Yikes!

It was like he knew why I had gone to law school. I went to law school because I had a vague idea that lawyers drive BMWs and live in big houses and have swimming pools. His point was that driving a BMW is not necessarily a bad thing and neither is living in a big house with a swimming pool. But if we spend our lives seeking money and don't use that money to bless the lives of other people who are poor or sick or captive, we will go to hell.

Now, you might not believe in a literal hell. I think Judge Griffith does, but you'd have to ask him. I believe in a literal hell. But even if you don't, I think his point is still valuable. Selfishness is not a road to happiness or fulfillment.

Many religious and philosophical traditions teach variations of this theme. In the New Testament, Jesus tells his disciples to "seek ye first the kingdom of God, and his righteousness; and all these things shall be added unto to you" (KJV Matt. 6:33). For Jesus, the kingdom of God included loving one another, healing the sick, and caring for the poor and the excluded.

In *Man's Search for Meaning*, Viktor E. Frankl relates his experience of finding meaning in the intense suffering of the Auschwitz concentration camp. As he marches with fellow prisoners and is driven forward by guards with rifles, he begins to think of his wife.

> Occasionally I looked at the sky, where the stars were fading and the pink light of the morning was beginning to spread behind a dark bank of clouds. But my mind clung to

my wife's image, imagining it with an uncanny acuteness. I heard her answering me, saw her smile, her frank and encouraging look. Real or not, her look was then more luminous than the sun which was beginning to rise.

Frankl had an epiphany in that concentration camp: "*The salvation of man is through love and in love.*" This might seem trite, but it was an insight Frankl gained at incredible cost. Focusing on his own pain and his own suffering was essentially a dead end. Only by focusing on something outside himself and more important than himself, could Frankl endure and find meaning in his suffering. In other words, "Those who have a 'why' to live, can bear with almost any 'how.'"

Obviously, enduring a concentration camp has little to do with practicing law. But Frankl's fundamental insight holds. A selfish and inward-focused attitude will lead to misery. While a person who focuses on something greater than themselves can find meaning in any circumstance.

I don't know enough about many other faith or philosophical traditions to draw meaningful conclusions about their teachings on selfishness. But my experience is that Judge Griffith, Jesus, and Frankl are all correct. If we are focused on ourselves, we will create our own personal hell no matter how wonderful our circumstances. When we focus on blessing and lifting those around us and we have a higher purpose, we can create a slice of heaven no matter where we are because we will be heavenly people.

Those words are easy to say or to write, but they are difficult to apply in the real world. We are all basically selfish people by nature and I am no exception. I have a lot of work to do to apply the lessons I have just written. But I take heart that I am doing better than I did in the past. When I am focused on serving and helping those around me, I am a better and a happier person.

Your law practice doesn't have to be hell. It can be meaningful and bring you joy. But the great paradox is that if you focus on your own happiness, your own wants and needs, you will be miserable.

"For whosoever will save his life shall lose it" (KJV Matt. 16:25). Your own happiness cannot be the goal of your practice or your life, or you will lose it. But if you lose yourself in a higher selfless purpose, happiness will be a necessary if unintentional byproduct.

Imagine the happiest person you know. No really. Stop for a minute and think about them. Who are you thinking about? What do they do? What differences are there between the way they live their life and the way you live yours?

The first three parts of this book were intended to provide practical principles that anyone can apply to create a law practice that they enjoy and is financially successful. But that is not enough to become a happy lawyer. There are plenty of lawyers who make tons of money and are miserable. Many lawyers tackle difficult and interesting problems all day. And yet they are unhappy.

The real goal isn't to make tons of money or to have a practice we enjoy. Obviously, those are very nice things. If you are broke and sweating your mortgage every month it is going to be very difficult to be happy or to be of service to anyone. If you despise the work you do all day, you might not have any energy left to serve your family or your community. But making money and enjoying your practice are not the final goal. What we really want is to be happy people and to make the world a better place. When your practice is successful and enjoyable you are better able to do those things. But we need to be careful to avoid mistaking those intermediary goals for the final purpose of our life.

I chose to put this Part at the end of this book, but I could have as easily put it first because the principles that lead to true happiness do not need to wait until after your practice is settled and financially successful. In fact, if you wait until your practice is successful to apply these principles, it may be much more difficult because you may have created bad habits that lead to unhappiness. But no matter where you are in your journey of making a practice and a life that you enjoy, you can apply these principles to lead a happier, more fulfilling, and more valuable life. They are not new principles or principles that I discovered or created. But if we do not deliberately look for ways to apply them, we will be unhappy lawyers no matter how successful our law practices are.

I know that it is possible for you to be happy. Even though law practice is not set up to make lawyers happy and even though you may have learned habits that actually make you unhappy, I believe that human beings can be happy if they apply correct principles in their lives. I hope these principles are helpful to you in your life and in your practice.

Conclusion

I hope this book is helpful to you. I hope it has encouraged you to start your own firm. Please don't try to create a firm that looks just like mine. The world deserves something better that has never existed before. Yours should be a reflection of your personality and your talents. You wouldn't have the same passion for my firm that I do and I wouldn't have the same passion as you do for your firm. Have the courage to experiment and create something great.

Use this book to start a conversation with yourself. If reading this book has sparked some ideas and motivated you to move closer to creating the practice of your dreams then it has achieved its goal. I know that you can do it. I had no idea what I was doing when I started my firm. I was a 25-year old history major with a law degree and a year of misdemeanor prosecution. I didn't have any clients or any leads. But I have created a firm that has earned millions of dollars in legal fees, served hundreds of clients, and allowed me to take care of my family. It has allowed me to shape my practice so that it is a reflection of my authentic self. I love my practice and I know you can build a practice you love too.

To build a practice you love and to be a happy criminal defense lawyer, you need to follow these four steps: First, figure out what kind of practice you love. It takes trial and error, but when you find it, you will be very glad you searched for it. Second, you have to pay the price to get very good at it. That means practicing deliberately and identifying the skills that are most important to your practice. It also means getting enough repetitions that you are an expert. Third, you need to position yourself as an expert who is qualified to charge premium fees. Charging those fees will signal to your clients that you are an expert and that they can trust you with their case. It will also liberate you to pick and choose your cases, do pro bono work, or donate to worthy causes. Finally, you need to find meaning in your life by serving others. You might choose to serve through pro bono work, taking care of your family, or donating money to groups that help the poor. But you won't be happy if you focus only on yourself.

I feel incredibly blessed to be a happy criminal defense lawyer. I want you to be a happy criminal defense lawyer too.

If you need a sounding board, have questions about something in this book, or want to know the best place to buy a sandwich in Salt Lake City, drop me a line at baron.josh@gmail.com.

Now go create something great.

Bonus Chapter: Marketing for Criminal Defense Lawyers

The first month after I started my law firm was nerve wracking. I would be home in the middle of the day playing video games. My wife would ask, "Why aren't you at work?" I would say, "I don't have any clients. I can play video games at the office or I can play them here."

She asked me to play video games at the office.

How do you get your first client? Once you have a stream of clients, how do you get more of the right clients who are willing to pay what you're worth and who need help with the problems you can solve?

Within one week of putting up your firm website, I guarantee that you will start getting offers from marketers who will help you "generate leads," "help you rank #1 on Google," and "get you more clients." Some of these people are probably helpful, but most will charge you thousands of dollars without delivering much of anything. How do you know what type of marketing to invest in? How do you know how much to spend? How can you tell if it is all working?

You can divide marketing opportunities into three categories: awareness marketing, targeted marketing, and referral marketing. Each has a role for a certain type of firm, but my suggestion is that for criminal defense firms, referral marketing is better than targeted marketing and targeted marketing is much much much better than awareness marketing.

Referral > Targeted > Awareness
Awareness Marketing

Whether you are the type of lawyer who has always wanted a billboard or the type who would never be caught dead with a late-night television commercial, awareness marketing can be very dangerous for small criminal defense firms. Awareness marketing is wide net advertising. It probably works or Coca Cola and McDonald's wouldn't spend so much money on it. But almost every single person who sees a Coca Cola commercial is a potential customer for Coca Cola. If you drink liquids, you could buy and drink Coke. Your potential market of criminal defendants is much smaller. Only a tiny percentage of people will be charged with a crime in any one year. A television commercial will reach thousands or millions of people who have no need of your services. And you will pay to reach each of them even though they don't need or want you.

But, you may say, personal injury attorneys spend tons of money on television commercials and billboards. They must work. All the other criminal defense lawyers are just too dumb to use them. You are different. Commercials and billboards will work for you. Besides, you have a great concept for a cool ad that will destroy the competition. In fact, you minored in advertising in undergad.

Personal injury attorneys use billboards and commercials for three reasons: First, a single personal injury case could be worth millions of dollars. It probably won't be. But there is a chance and personal injury attorneys are willing to take the risk. Second, there isn't always a really good way to reach potential car accident victims at the moment they are looking for a lawyer. Sure, they might google "car accident lawyer" when they get back from the hospital. But by that time, they may have already signed a settlement and release with the insurance company. And third, car accidents are pretty evenly distributed among the whole population. So while most people don't get in a car accident in a given year, poor people, rich people, young people, old people, and people of different ethnic groups are about equally likely to be involved in a serious accident.

Those things are not true for criminal defense lawyers. No one case is likely to be worth millions of dollars. There are good ways to target your prospective clients. And you know where they are and who they are when they get charged with a crime.

To put it into military terms, awareness marketing is like long-range artillery. It's nice. It makes the infantry's job easier. But you can't win a war with artillery alone. You need boots on the ground.

Awareness marketing is sexy. It sounds so easy. " Four million people pass this billboard every year." You think to yourself, "If just 1% of those people call me and hire me, that billboard will pay for itself in like 39 seconds." But 1% of people who pass a billboard won't call the number on it. Awareness marketing builds awareness. It does not drive immediate conversions. It takes time and repetition to build awareness. It takes an expensive, long-term, focused commitment to break through the noise of advertising. And, again, very few of the people who pass that billboard will ever need you. They might want a Coke or Nike shoes or a McDonald's hamburger. Let those companies buy a billboard. You are too smart for that.

Targeted Marketing

Targeted marketing is better than awareness marketing. At least for small law firms. You don't have millions of dollars to spend or years to wait for awareness marketing to pay off. I started my firm with a few hundred dollars. That meant that I needed clients the first month to pay me money so that I could pay the rent for the next month. You are probably in a similar situation. There isn't much margin for error. You have to know how well your marketing is working quickly. That's where targeted marketing comes in handy.

When I started my firm, I couldn't afford Google Adwords. My partner and I sent direct mailers to the addresses of people who had been charged with crimes. We sent them the same day they were charged and we sent them to the address they listed on the court website. It was targeted advertising because we knew that these people needed our services right then. We weren't spending money on every single person in Salt Lake County who passed a billboard. We were spending money on the few hundred people who were charged with crimes every day. It was relatively expensive and time consuming to send our direct mailer to each person. The paper and envelopes and postage cost about 60 cents per mailer. We manually copied and pasted each address into a mail merge and stuffed the envelopes by hand ourselves. But we knew that these were people who were likely to need our services at that moment. The mailers were a huge success. They launched our firm.

We knew exactly how many mailers we sent each day, how many people called us, and how many of those people hired us. We could easily measure the effectiveness of the mailers and be sure that it was worth our time and money. We could adjust the offers, the typeface, the copy in the letter and see what worked best. It wasn't glamorous, but it worked. Utah allows direct-mail advertising, but not every state does. Make sure you follow your state's advertising rules.

As we have gained experience and positioned ourselves as experts, we have stopped sending direct mailers. We spend more of our time and money on Adwords. The principle is the same, though. If you search, "How long will I lose my license if I get a felony DUI," there's a good chance you also need a criminal defense lawyer. I know how many people call us, how many call because they found us online, and how much those people pay us. So, I know how much we can afford to pay for online advertising. At the time these potential clients most need my services, I am introducing myself online and telling them I can help them solve their criminal defense problem.

As you evaluate expensive marketing opportunities, look for measurable advertising. Look for a short feedback loop between the time you spend the money and when you find out whether the client hired you. In five years, you might start direct mailers or stop Adwords. Some new technology might be available that is more targeted than either and it might be cheaper or more expensive. As long as you can measure the effectiveness of your advertising and as long as there is a quick feedback loop telling you what works before you're bankrupt, you should experiment until you find really effective targeted advertising.

Referral Marketing

Targeted advertising is good. Referral marketing is even better. When I was little, my dad was involved in real estate management and development. It was very lucrative and my mom enjoyed his income. When I was about 10 years old, he decided to become a teacher. Teaching is a less lucrative field. My mom missed his real estate income. So, she bought him a subscription to the Wall Street Journal and said, "You have to make one call a day." She called it the one-call-a-day program. My dad's assignment was to read the Journal until he found an article that someone he knew might be interested in. Then, he had to call that person and say, "Hey, I was reading this article and I thought you might like it. By the way, how are things?" Then he got off the phone within a few minutes so that these people didn't dread his calls.

He wasn't selling anything. He wasn't asking for anything. He was just staying in touch in a genuine way with people he already knew and liked. Within a short time, one of the people he called said, "Thanks so much for calling. I need to invest $1,000,000 in Southern California real estate. Can you help me find the right deals?" The one-call-a-day program works.

I knew about the one-call-a-day program when I started my firm, but I thought it didn't apply to lawyers because we can't do in-person solicitation.

It's true that you can't solicit potential clients. But, like my dad, you can call or stay in touch with people without asking for anything. You could read the Wall Street Journal and call other lawyers and say, "I saw this and I thought of you." It will come up that you are a criminal defense lawyer.

Think about the people who can be potential referral sources for your criminal defense firm. Other lawyers who don't do criminal defense are looking for someone to refer to. They have friends and family members bugging them to help with a DUI or a theft case. Help them think of you when those people ask them. A friend introduced me to a guy my age who went to law school but doesn't practice law. Over the years, he has referred me a number of good cases defending his friends and co-workers. Plus, he's a great friend and an interesting guy to have lunch with.

Other criminal defense lawyers will have conflicts of interest. In my practice, this happens most often with co-defendants. If the marijuana was on the console of the car and the husband was driving with the wife in the passenger seat, I can't represent both. Each one's best defense is that the prosecution can't prove the other wasn't possessing the marijuana. So stay in touch with other criminal defense lawyers. If they ask you to cover a hearing for them, do it. One of my former employees has a successful defense practice. Recently, he asked me if I'd like some Jazz tickets. I love NBA games, but my wife isn't really excited to use our family's money to buy expensive tickets. This friend gave me three great games last season. When I have a co-defendant to refer, he is the first person I think of. I have referred him tens of thousands of dollars-worth of cases.

One of my best sources of referrals is a bail bondsman. I didn't consciously try to cultivate him as a referral source. One of his family members hired us without him knowing it. We did a good job for them and he started being a walking billboard for our firm. He has referred some of my best clients to me and they always start out with an extremely favorable opinion of me before I do anything. Recently, he had a friend with a complicated problem with a pawnbroker who was going to sell some family guns. He called me and asked if I could help out. I said, "Of course." I researched the pawn laws, which I knew nothing about, and wrote a demand letter. We were able to get the guns back and avoid further pawn fees. It was the least I could do for someone who has been so generous to me over the years.

You never know who could refer you a case. Do great work. Be kind to people. Don't be a jerk even if you feel like being a jerk. Consciously build a network of people you genuinely like and care about. Serve them. Don't think about what they are going to do for you. Just try to help them and be a nice person. Over time, no amount of advertising will overcome a bad reputation and a good reputation will be way more valuable than any billboard or TV commercial.

If I could go back and give myself one piece of advice when I started my firm, it would be to do more contacting. Not weirdo "networking" and handing out business cards. But send a thank you note. Send a letter to someone saying you noticed how well they did something. Do someone a favor.

Be kind. Remember their birthday. Don't solicit clients. But consciously schedule time to stay in touch with people you might be tempted to drift away from. And posting something on Facebook doesn't count.

Good marketing can't fix a bad law firm. But good law firms die all the time because they did a bad job of talking to their potential clients. Find cost-effective and genuine ways to reach out to new clients. Do great work for them, and you'll be successful. Building your dream criminal defense firm is scary. But it's not really dangerous. You won't actually starve. You might have to work hard. You might have lean months. But if a clueless history major who failed as a standup comedian can do it, you can too.

Just do it. We need you.

Made in the USA
Monee, IL
12 September 2021